A Gift for You Compliments of

Trafford Library
416 Brinton Ave.
Trafford, PA 15085
412-372-5115

This edition first published in MMXVII by
Book House

Distributed by Black Rabbit Books
P.O. Box 3263
Mankato
Minnesota MN 56002

Cataloging-in-Publication Data is available
from the Library of Congress

Printed in the United States
At Corporate Graphics,
North Mankato, Minnesota

9 8 7 6 5 4 3 2 1

ISBN: 978-1-910706-91-6

EXPLORERS

The Story of
MARCO POLO

Jacqueline Morley David Antram

BOOK HOUSE

CONTENTS

INTRODUCTION

Marco Polo was born in Italy, in 1254. When he died in 1324, aged 70, he could look back on a lifetime of extraordinary adventures, traveling across half the known world in the service of the formidable Mongol emperor, Kublai Khan. On his journeys, Marco Polo explored rich cities and fabulous palaces, admired spectacular scenery, and met fascinating local peoples. None had been seen by Europeans before. Marco Polo had his amazing adventures written down. If his book is true—and scholars think it probably is—he traveled farther, and saw more, than anyone ever before.

Although Marco Polo faced many dangers on his journeys, he lived at a time when travel across Asia was safe—at least by medieval standards. This was because the Mongols, fierce nomad soldiers led by warrior Chingiz Khan (died 1227), had conquered a vast empire, stretching from Turkey to China. The Mongols were ruthless invaders, but they brought law and order to the lands they ruled.

MARCO POLO'S HOME TOWN

Marco Polo was born in Venice—a rich, powerful city in northern Italy. Venice was a port and its wealth came from trade. Like many other Venetian citizens, Marco Polo's family were merchants, making a living by buying and selling goods. Sailing ships from countries all round the Mediterranean sea docked in the lagoon— Venice's shallow, sheltered harbor. They were loaded with valuable cargoes from distant lands: glassware, pottery, fine metalware, Chinese ceramics, porcelain, and ornate bronzes. Venice was also the major port for ships sailing to Europe from the Black Sea.

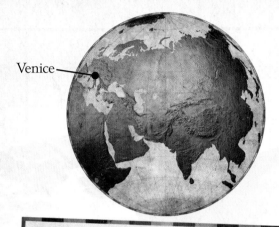

Venice

The Waterfront

Venice was built on a cluster of islands, linked by bridges, in a shallow, marshy lagoon. Ships could unload their cargoes at its long waterfront, right in the city center.

Traders bargained to get the best prices for goods they had brought from overseas.

A RICH TRADING CITY

Only rich merchants could afford a house like the Polos' family home in Venice. It was built on several floors, with doorways and windows decorated with the latest designs.

It was spacious and well-heated. Rooms were candle-lit and had tapestry wall-hangings, rush mats, and wooden chests. Merchants entertained customers at home, hoping they might buy more!

The Polos' home

Shops and Streets

The city streets were lined with market stalls and booths where bankers, money-changers, and money-lenders did business. Rich merchants had shops and showrooms in their homes.

INTERNATIONAL TRADE

Valuable goods from the Far East reached European ports, like Venice, by two different routes. The "Silk Road" ran overland, from China to the shores of the Black Sea. The "Spice Route" stretched across the sea from China and the Spice Islands (in present-day Indonesia), then over the Indian Ocean to the Red Sea and the Persian Gulf.

Few traders traveled the length of the Silk Road or the Spice Route. Instead, they made purchases from merchants in neighboring lands. Goods were often bought and sold several times on their long journeys across land and sea.

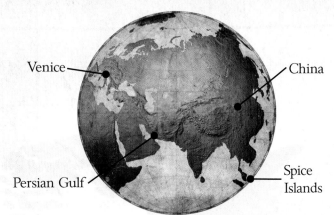

Venice — China

Persian Gulf — Spice Islands

Silk-making

Silk-making was a closely-guarded secret in China. Threads from silkworm cocoons were unwound, woven on a hand-loom, and dyed in bright colors.

Merchants and their families liked to wear fashionable clothes.

THE SILK ROAD AND THE SPICE ROUTE

The map below shows the Silk Road and the Spice Route. Travelers making long journeys often had to pay high tolls to local rulers before being allowed to continue their journey. They added these charges to the price of the goods they were carrying, making them even more expensive.

Exotic spices:

Favorite spices imported into Europe from India and the Spice Islands: 1. Ginger 2. Nutmeg 3. Mace 4. Black pepper 5. Cloves 6. Cinnamon

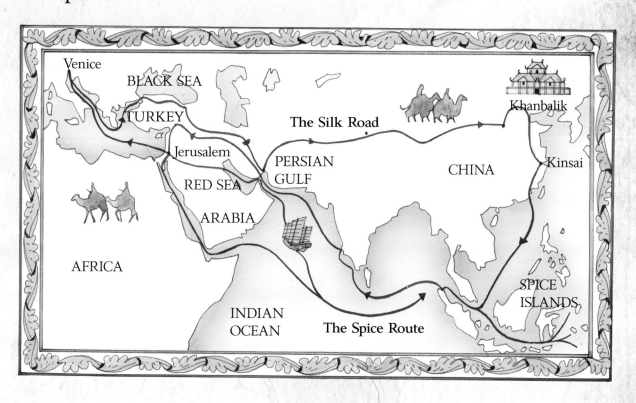

Bartering

Craft workers and foreign merchants used different currencies, and were often suspicious of the value of each other's coins. Many goods were exchanged for food, horses, or other valuable items, instead.

MONGOL LORDS OF ASIA

In 1260, Marco Polo's father, Niccolo, and uncle, Maffeo, made a bold decision. They would travel east themselves, maybe to China, and stock up with valuable silks and jewels to sell on their return. The trip would be long and risky. They did not return home until 1268.

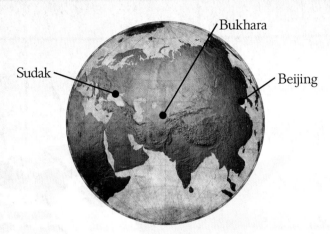
Bukhara
Sudak
Beijing

The Mongols were brave fighters. They conquered an empire which stretched from Hungary to Korea.

From Europe to Asia

The Polos sailed from Constantinople and then across the Black Sea to Sudak in the Crimea (present-day Ukraine). In Central Asia their progress was halted by a war between Mongol tribes.

THE OLDER POLOS MEET KUBLAI KHAN

In the Central Asian city of Bukhara the Polos took refuge from the Mongols' civil war. They joined a group of merchants setting off for China and the court of Kublai Khan (who ruled from 1260 to 1294).

Kublai Khan gave the Polos a gold paitze (like a passport) so they could travel home safely.

Clothes against the Cold
The Mongols were nomadic tribes that lived in tents called "yurts." They wore long sheepskin coats, and trousers for warmth.

Khanbalik
Finally, they reached the Mongols' capital city in China at Khanbalik (present-day Beijing). The Kublai Khan welcomed them at his palace. He was very interested in Europeans.

THE ADVENTURE BEGINS

Niccolo and Maffeo Polo had promised Kublai Khan they would return. So in 1271 they set off again for China, taking seventeen-year-old Marco with them. For Marco, it was the start of a lifetime of adventure. He did not see his home again for over 20 years. The Polos sailed from Venice across the Mediterranean Sea. They arrived in Acre, a busy port in the Holy Land, just south of the present-day city of Beirut in Lebanon.

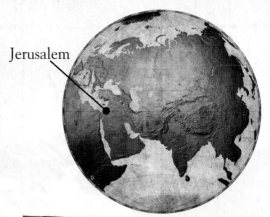

Jerusalem

The city of Jerusalem (below) was holy to Christians, Jews, and Muslims. Since 1095 Christians and Muslims had fought over who had the right to rule it.

Sea Travel

Sea journeys were hazardous then. Travelers braved storms, shipwrecks, and pirate attacks. But for merchants and adventurers the rewards could be great.

Jerusalem

At the Holy Sepulchre (Jesus's tomb) in Jerusalem, the Polos collected a flask of holy oil to take as a present to Kublai Khan. Then they headed east, traveling through wild countryside with prosperous towns and beautiful buildings along the way.

MARCO POLO LEAVES HOME

Camel Caravans

In the deserts of Iran and Central Asia, the Polos met merchants' caravans with camels loaded with goods.

Wherever the Polos traveled on their way to China, they had to get permission to travel through certain lands from local governors and officials. Many people suspected that the Polos might be spies.

In Konya, eastern Turkey, the Polos passed the beautiful Ince Minareli Madrasa (Muslim college), built in 1258.

Travels

On the shores of the Caspian Sea, the Polos saw natural oil wells. Marco Polo commented on the fine horses in Iran and the beautiful, brilliantly-colored ceramics he saw there (right).

STRANGE VOICES

It took the Polo family over three years to travel to China. They had to cross rivers and swamps in Iraq, dangerously high mountains in the Hindu Kush, and deserts in Mongolia. Often, they had to wait for the right weather. In winter, mountain passes were blocked with snow, and in summer, the desert sands burned travelers' feet. They faced frost-bite, heat-stroke, hunger, thirst, and robbers and bandits, too.

Everywhere Marco Polo went, he looked and listened, asked questions, and observed people. He tried new foods, new clothes, and made new friends.

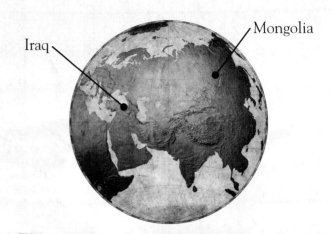

Iraq

Mongolia

Learning Languages
On his travels, Marco Polo met many different Central Asian peoples. He learned to speak four Asian languages, including Chinese and Turki, languages spoken by the Mongols.

Travelers had to pass through high mountain ranges and rough terrain. It took 30 days just to cross the Gobi desert.

THE DANGER AND DELIGHT OF TRAVEL

The desert winds quickly covered travelers' tracks. It was easy to get lost. Travelers in the desert feared meeting mischievous spirits called djinns, who wailed and cried in the night. By day, djinns disguised themselves as people, then led travelers astray so they got lost.

There were also reports of the sounds of a long-dead, ghostly army, marching off to war. They heard the thunder of horses' hooves, and the shouts and cries of battle. This made them very afraid.

Ghost Towns
After crossing the Pamir Mountains, between present-day China and Pakistan, the Polos rode to the oasis at Kashgar.
Traveling on, they passed eerie, deserted towns covered by sand. It was a relief to arrive at Khotan.

Overnight stop around a campfire. It was sometimes possible to sleep in the safety of "khans"—travelers' rest houses.

TENTS AND PALACES

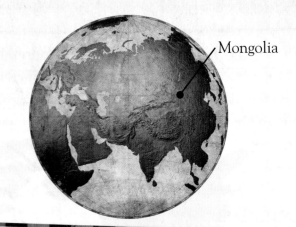

Mongolia

The Polos' journey now took them across Mongolia to meet the Mongol emperor at his summer palace in Shangdu, north of Beijing. When the Polos reached the palace, they presented Kublai Khan with the holy oil they had brought from Jerusalem. He was very pleased. Kublai greeted the travelers warmly, and held a lavish feast.

Marco had never seen anything to equal the richness and splendor of Kublai's court. He described the opulence of the emperor's hunting tent, his vast herds of horses, and the feats performed by magicians and healers who lived at the summer palace.

Silken Tent

When he was out hunting, Kublai Khan rested in a splendid tent. It was made of silk and spice-wood, decorated with carved dragons, and ornamented with gold. Inside, it was lined with lion-skins and other expensive furs.

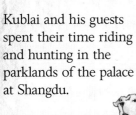

Kublai and his guests spent their time riding and hunting in the parklands of the palace at Shangdu.

AT THE MONGOL EMPEROR'S COURT

Kublai Khan had four chief wives and 22 sons. He had another 25 sons by his unofficial wives. Daughters are not mentioned. Kublai Khan entertained hundreds of guests at great feasts in the grounds of his summer palace. Some guests were Mongols, others were Chinese.

Kublai Khan's Palace

Each summer, Kublai Khan spent three months at his magnificent palace of marble and precious stones.

Feasting in the palace grounds

Magicians

Magicians and healers from Tibet and Kashmir lived in Kublai Khan's palace at Shangdu. Marco Polo claimed that they used spells to drive away rain-clouds so that the weather around the palace was always fine.

KUBLAI KHAN

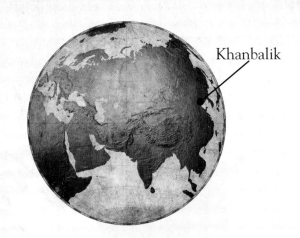

Khanbalik

K ublai Khan spent most of his life fighting. (He did not finally conquer all of China until 1279.) The lands he had conquered were guarded at key points by fierce Mongol soldiers. Kublai Khan built a new capital city at Khanbalik (modern Beijing). According to Polo, its palace was "the largest ever seen." The territory conquered by warrior Chingiz Khan was divided into four khanates (empires). Kublai ruled the largest, eastern khanate: China, Mongolia, Tibet, and nearby lands. Within his empire, Kublai had absolute power. He introduced Mongol laws and collected heavy taxes, but allowed people to follow their own religion and way of life.

Kublai Khan holds court.

Governors

Kublai Khan appointed governors for all of the provinces in his vast empire. If they disobeyed him, they were killed.

A RULER WITH ABSOLUTE POWER

Mongol armies besieged many great cities during Kublai Khan's conquest of China. They camped outside city walls, trying to smash their way in using siege engines, or simply waiting for the trapped inhabitants to starve.

Messengers

Relays of riders carried urgent orders. Staging posts along the main roads provided food and fresh horses.

Mongol Money

The Chinese were skilled paper makers. Marco Polo was very impressed by the banknotes he saw being used in China. Paper money was a Mongol invention.

CHINESE LANDS

According to Marco Polo, Kublai Khan was the "mightiest man in the world today, in subjects, territory, and treasure." The densely-populated Chinese lands ruled by Kublai Khan were home to one of the richest, most advanced civilizations in the world. Chinese engineers designed and built wide, paved roads, graceful bridges, thousands of miles of canals, and complex irrigation schemes. Marco Polo admired its prosperous cities, fine palaces and temples, beautiful gardens, and wonderful decorative objects. He was greatly impressed by many inventions unknown in European lands.

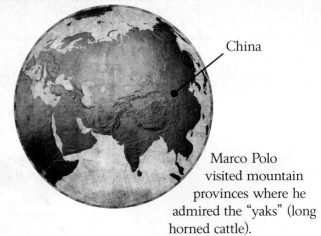

China

Marco Polo visited mountain provinces where he admired the "yaks" (long horned cattle).

Farming in China

Farmers grew wheat, soy beans, and melons in the fertile soils of north China. In the south, they grew rice in flooded "paddy" fields. They bred ducks and geese, and harvested plentiful crops of vegetables.

CHINESE CIVILIZATION

Fishing

Fishermen on the Yangtze River used specially-trained cormorants (diving birds) to catch fish for them. A ring around the bird's throat stopped it swallowing its catch.

Innovations

Irrigation channels brought water to the fields, and sluices and barriers protected the land from floods. Chinese wheelbarrows, invented around AD 200, were much easier to push than European ones. Treadmills were used to pump water upward from streams.

CITY OF HEAVEN

Marco Polo reported that the city of Kinsai (present-day Hangzhou) was the "finest and most splendid in the world." Kinsai was the capital of the central region of China, and the largest city in Kublai's empire. Marco visited it several times. Kinsai had grown rich through trade. Rich merchants bought and sold silks, medicines, and spices. Its craft workers produced exquisite silk fabric, lacquerware, and jewelry. The citizens wore fine clothes and held lavish parties. Marco reported that people ate fish and meat (both expensive luxuries) at the same meal.

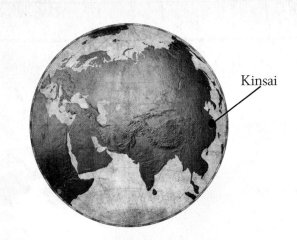

Kinsai

Busy market place

Bridges

Marco Polo said there were 12,000 bridges in Kinsai. This was probably an exaggeration, but since the Chinese were expert bridge-builders, there were no doubt several hundred bridges across the city's rivers, canals, and lake.

MARCO VISITS KINSAI

There were ten big markets in Kinsai and countless small, local ones. They sold "everything that could be wished to sustain life." Marco Polo was astonished at all the wonderful fruit and many kinds of fish that could be bought in these markets. The fish were caught in the city's lake where they grew fat eating trash.

Bathhouses

Marco Polo was impressed by the public bathhouses in Kinsai. Local people bathed daily in cold water, for hygiene and health. There were warm water baths for foreigners who could not stand cold water.

Banquets were held by the lakeside. Kinsai had a huge lake, with summer-houses and palaces all round the shore.

City Guilds

According to Marco Polo there were 12 craft guilds in Kinsai, each with 12,000 workshops employing between 10 and 40 people. Some city streets housed scholars who taught reading and writing, or astrologers who cast horoscopes and foretold the future.

SOUTHEAST ASIA

Marco's father and uncle seem to have spent most of their time in China working as traders, but Marco was sent on long journeys to distant parts of Kublai's empire as a messenger, or perhaps a spy. He visited many remote regions, including Tibet, Burma (present-day Myanmar,) Bengal (present-day Bangladesh), and Laos—where he marveled at people who coated their teeth with solid gold and who covered their bodies with tattoos.

On his journeys, Marco met other travelers who told him tales of amazing things they had seen. Some of these travelers' tales may have been exaggerated, but many of them were true.

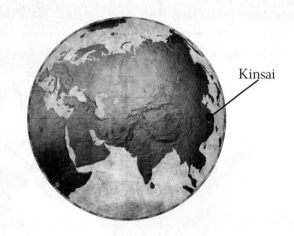

Kinsai

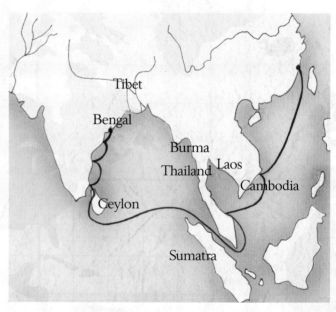

Marco spent many years traveling in South-East Asia. In his book he described many of the countries he visited. These descriptions form a valuable historical record.

Pearl Fishers

Off the coasts of Ceylon and eastern India, Marco Polo watched divers search underwater for oysters containing pearls.

MARCO EXPLORES NEARBY LANDS

In Ceylon (present-day Sri Lanka), Marco met Buddhist monks who had sent holy relics as gifts to Kublai Khan. In India, he admired the young women who danced in front of statues of gods and goddesses in Hindu temples. They also offered the statues food and garlands of flowers. He heard stories in Cambodia of King Jayavarman who paid Kublai Khan tribute of several war elephants—and had 326 children!

In Burma, Marco Polo traveled past Buddhist and gold-covered stupas (Buddhist shrines) like this one at Mingalazedi.

Weird Creatures

In Sumatra, Indonesia, Marco described "very ugly brutes," which he said were unicorns. They were probably black rhinoceroses.
In Sumatra, Marco Polo saw "men with tails." In fact, they were orangutans, a species of apes that lives in the rain forests there.

THE JOURNEY HOME

After traveling in the East for over 20 years, the Polos wanted to go home. Marco was nearing 40 and his father and uncle were old men. But they could not leave China without Kublai Khan's permission. By great good fortune, a troop of soldiers, courtiers, and servants were getting ready to leave Kublai's court, as escorts to a Mongol princess traveling to marry a ruler in the Middle East. The overland route was blocked by war, so the Polos volunteered to act as guides for the journey by sea.

They set off in 1292. The sea voyage to the Middle East took 18 months and was full of dangers. Marco said that out of 700 people on board, only 117 survived. Once Princess Kokachin was safely escorted to her bridegroom, the Polos continued on their journey homeward. Nine months later, in 1295, they finally reached Venice.

Venice ——— ——— China

The Polos finally returned home after over 24 years.

Strangers

Arriving back in Venice, dirty and shabby-looking, no one recognized the Polos. They ripped open the seams of their Mongol-style clothes to reveal the jewels hidden inside. At last everyone believed them.

TELLING THE TALE

Everyone welcomed the Polos home. Their family thought they had all died long ago.

In 1298, Venice went to war with Genoa. Marco was captured and put in prison. There, he met a writer called Rustichello of Pisa.

Marco told him stories about his many travels. Rustichello turned Marco Polo's stories into a book. It soon became very popular and was translated into many different languages to be sold far and wide.

True story?

Marco Polo may have exaggerated some of his adventures and Rustichello may have added some "extra" episodes of his own. (He had written mostly romances before.) But historians have checked many of the details about people and places in the book. It seems as if most of Marco's story is probably true.

We know very little about the last years of Marco Polo's life, after he was set free from prison in 1299. Only two pieces of evidence survive. One is a manuscript which calls him by his nickname, "Il Milione" (Mr. Million.) We do not know why he was called this—perhaps because of his boastful talk about his travels, perhaps because of the treasures he brought home with him. The second, and last, piece of evidence is Marco's will, made shortly before his death in 1324. In this, he mentions that he has three daughters, and leaves them a substantial amount of money—though not an enormous fortune. This suggests that Marco had perhaps exaggerated the amount of treasures he had brought back with him to Venice. In his will, Marco also mentions his servant, Peter, who came from the Tatars (a Mongol tribe). Marco gives instructions that when he dies, Peter should be set free.

WHAT HAPPENED NEXT?

Marco Polo, his father and his uncle, were among the first to make the difficult and dangerous journey right along the Silk Road. But they were also among the last to do so for almost 500 years.

The last medieval European we know about who visited China was another Italian merchant, named Francesco Balducci Pegolotti. He went there in about 1340 and wrote a guide for other travelers called The Merchants' Handbook. It is not as entertaining and enjoyable as Marco Polo's book, but Pegolotti does make one interesting comment: "the road from the Black Sea to China is now perfectly safe, by day or by night."

In 1320, a Christian missionary, Fra Odoric of Pordenone, set out for China hoping to spread the Christian faith. We do not know whether he ever met Marco Polo, or knew of Marco's book. If he had read it, he would have discovered from Marco's descriptions that very few people in Asia knew about Christianity in the 1260s or 1270s. But by 1307, the situation had changed. In that year, the Pope appointed the first Roman Catholic Bishop of Beijing. This suggests there was a sizable Christian community living there, and that several Christian missionaries may have been working in northern China in Marco Polo's time. In the book he wrote around 1330 about his journey to China, Odoric remarked, "there are now many people in Venice who have visited Kinsai."

But this period of peaceful and successful travel did not last long. In 1368 the Chinese people rebelled against their Mongol rulers, drove them out of the country, and set up a new ruling family of their own. Under these new rulers—called the Ming Dynasty—foreigners were not welcome to visit China. Brave, adventurous, profitable journeys, like the one pioneered by Marco Polo and his family, would not be possible again for hundreds of years.

GLOSSARY

Barter
To exchange goods of equal value.

Bronze
A mixture of copper and tin, used to make decorative objects, containers, and ceremonial swords.

Caravans
Herds of specially-trained camels, used to carry heavy loads for long distances over dry or desert land.

Ceramics
Items made from clay, especially pottery, tiles, and porcelain.

Empire
Many nations joined together under the rule of a single leader called an emperor.

Frost-bite
Damage to skin (especially nose, fingers, and toes) caused by extreme cold.

Heat-stroke
Illness caused by too much exposure to hot sun. Sufferers have a raised temperature and a severe headache.

Nomadic
People who move their homes from place to place, in search of food and water for themselves and, sometimes, their herds of animals.

Sluice
An underwater gate that regulates the flow of water passing through it.

Khan (i)
Mongol word for ruler.

Yurt
Mongol tent, made of felt on a wooden frame.

Khan (ii)
Public rest-house where travelers and their animals could stay safely overnight. Also called a "caravanserai."

Khanate
Lands ruled by a Khan.

Mongols
Nomad peoples who lived in Central Asia and present-day Mongolia. They were brave fighters and expert horse-riders. In the 13th century they conquered a vast empire, led by Chingiz and Kublai Khan.

INDEX